MW01267641

# The TRUE Fairy Tale

## Diane Mack

TRILOGY CHRISTIAN PUBLISHERS
*TUSTIN, CA*

Trilogy Christian Publishers
A Wholly Owned Subsidary of Trinity Broadcasting Network
2442 Michelle Drive
Tustin, CA 92780

10 9 8 7 6 5 4 3 2 1

Library of Congress Cataloging-in-Publication Data is available.

ISBN 978-1-64773-288-2

ISBN 978-1-64773-289-9

# Contents

Dedication.........................................................................v

Preface............................................................................vii

Introduction ....................................................................ix

Prologue .........................................................................xi

1. Protection in Times of Need...*Angels Abound* ............. 1

2. Falling Star...*God Answers Knee Mail* ........................... 5

3. Holding Hands...*In Training by the Holy Spirit* ..........15

4. As the Deer Pants for Streams of Water...
   *Aware of God's Presence and Truths* ............................ 27

5. In the Face of Adversity...*Staying in the
   Will of God* .................................................................31

6. Going Where I've Never Been Before...*Making
   it Through the Desert* .................................................. 35

7. Back Surgery...*Taking God Out of the Box* ................. 47

8. Attacked...*The Power of the Blood of Jesus* ................. 57

Epilogue ......................................................................... 67

Afterword ....................................................................... 77

Endnotes ........................................................................ 79

About the Author .......................................................... 83

# Dedication

To Mildred, who taught me by example to close my eyes to the world's distractions and focus only on Jesus.

To Walter, whose words, "Don't let your human mind limit God's power in your life," have guided my faith walk ever since hearing them.

And to Joyce, whose words, "Always be continually available to God," have helped me realize so many God-moments in my life.

*I purposely don't share their last names because there are many "Mildreds," "Walters," and "Joyces" in our lives, and this book is dedicated to all of them, whoever they may be.*

# Preface

Some people have the ability to share their hearts through music. If I tried, I would empty the room in mere seconds! In God's infinite wisdom, He knew this and had mercy on all of you. Instead, more than thirty years ago, He nudged me to begin writing notes so that I could one day share my heart in a book. In your hand is but a glimpse of how I have become part of His story.

# Introduction

Have you ever gazed up at the stars and questioned whether, or even how, a being called God could exist? When you hear His story, does it sound more like a fairy tale? Even as a believer in God's existence, have you ever had thoughts like these run through your mind? What is "faith" and how do we develop it? By reading The TRUE Fairy Tale, I hope that each reader will ponder where they are personally in God's story and discover His realness. Come, join me around the campfire to hear this amazing tale of love and grace found in the one true God.

# Prologue

*Once upon a time*, many, many moons ago, there was nothing—except God the Creator—the Alpha and the Omega, the Beginning and the End. And then, in His way and in His own time, God created the heavens and the earth. He created both light and dark and placed the moon and sun in the sky to rule over the night and day. The Creator continued to look at His canvas and pour forth His imagination. With a stroke of His brush, He brought forth all kinds of vegetation and living creatures on land, in the sky, and in the ocean. God looked at His creation and saw that it was good. We look around us and above us and see this to be true. The delicate balance and intricacies of all creation sing of His glory and existence!

In all that was good, God still yet had more to create—man in His own image to rule over all other creation.[1] It was a very intimate and powerful moment when God the Creator breathed life into His creation to become a living being. God blessed His creation, man and woman, whom He called Adam and Eve. He placed them in the "Garden of Eden," which means paradise of delight. Everything was created in perfection, and the needs of all living things were provided. "The LORD thy God in the midst of thee is mighty; he will save, he will rejoice over thee with joy; he will rest in his love, he will joy over thee with singing" (Zephaniah 3:17, KJV).

God the Creator became God the Father over mankind. His love for us was so great that He set us apart from all other creation by giving us a mind to reason and make free-will choices. God's desire was for mankind to choose to love Him in return to create a two-way relationship. He is a "gentleman" and does not force us into a relationship with Him.

As Adam and Eve walked in the garden, they knew God's Spirit was with them. God allowed them complete freedom with just one instruction—only one..."And the Lord God commanded the man, saying, "Of every tree of the garden thou mayest freely eat. But of the tree of the knowledge of good and evil, thou shalt not eat of it: for in the day that thou eatest thereof thou shalt surely die" (Genesis 2:16-17, KJV).

And then it happened! Adam and Eve chose to taste of the one thing they had been warned about, rather than be satisfied with the abundance that surrounded them![2] No, it wasn't the taste of money, sexual sin, abuse of drugs or alcohol, or any of the many things we have all been warned of and deal with in our world today, but the choice was the same. They made a conscious choice to taste of what they knew to be harmful...fruit from the tree of knowledge.

God did not want us to know evil. He did not want us to know death. His instruction is meant for good for us! He provided a perfect world for man, but to taste of "forbidden fruits" to satisfy temporary gratification is still a sin for us now just as much as it was for Adam and Eve. God's Word and commandments do not change with societal changes. God, just as much as a loving God, is a just God, but there are consequences for breaking His instruction.

With Adam and Eve's choice, their level of knowledge immediately changed; they became aware of their nakedness and were embarrassed. At that moment, mankind became separated from God's perfection as a result of—*not God's choice*—but the choice man made. It was man's choice to ignore God's counsel and turn their backs on God the Father. The relationship was broken; man would no longer enjoy the perfection of nature which God had intended. Adam and Eve were sent away from the garden where all had been provided for their enjoyment. They, and all of us to follow, now live a life working to provide for ourselves. We experience disease, death, crime, broken marriages, hatred, unforgiveness, and even more. *"Wherefore, as by one man sin entered into the world, and death by sin; and so death passed upon all men, for that all have sinned"* (Romans 5:12, KJV).

But wait! Because of the deep love of God the Father, our Creator, at the same time He announced punishment for man's choice of rejecting His perfect plan, He revealed His plan of grace that would model forgiveness! "God made Him who had no sin to be sin for us, so that in Him we might become the righteousness of God" (2 Corinthians 5:21, NIV).

Jesus, the Son of God, gave up His divine privileges and was born of a virgin as a newborn baby. "The Word became flesh and made his dwelling among us. We have seen his glory, the glory of the one and only Son, who came from the Father, full of grace and truth" (John 1:14, NIV). Jesus grew up to become the sacrificial lamb to bear our punishment for our sins.

While growing into a man, Jesus experienced both joy and sorrow just as we experience it each day. God understands our hearts as we go through these happy and sad times because His Son experienced them firsthand while here on earth. When Jesus' time came to begin His ministry to the world, He *knew* what He was going to have to suffer on His way to and on the cross, and by God's grace and deep love, He went willingly.

Then Pilate took Jesus and had him flogged. The soldiers twisted together a crown of thorns and put it on his head. They clothed him in a purple robe and went up to him again and again, saying, "Hail, king of the Jews!" And they slapped him in the face.

Once more Pilate came out and said to the Jews gathered there, "Look, I am bringing him out to you to let you know that I find no basis for a charge against him." When Jesus came out wearing the crown of thorns and the purple robe, Pilate said to them, "Here is the man!"

As soon as the chief priests and their officials saw him, they shouted, "Crucify! Crucify!"

But Pilate answered, "You take him and crucify him. As for me, I find no basis for a charge against him."

The Jewish leaders insisted, "We have a law, and according to that law he must die, because he claimed to be the Son of God."

When Pilate heard this, he was even more afraid, and he went back inside the palace. "Where do you come from?" he asked Jesus, but Jesus gave him no answer. "Do you refuse to speak to me?" Pilate said. "Don't you realize I have power either to free you or to crucify you?"

Jesus answered, "You would have no power over me if it were not given to you from above. Therefore the one who handed me over to you is guilty of a greater sin."

From then on, Pilate tried to set Jesus free, but the Jewish leaders kept shouting, "If you let this man go, you are no friend of Caesar. Anyone who claims to be a king opposes Caesar."

When Pilate heard this, he brought Jesus out and sat down on the judge's seat at a place known as the Stone Pavement (which in Aramaic is Gabbatha). It was the day of Preparation of the Passover; it was about noon.

"Here is your king," Pilate said to the Jews.

But they shouted, "Take him away! Take him away! Crucify him!"

"Shall I crucify your king?" Pilate asked.

"We have no king but Caesar," the chief priests answered.

Finally Pilate handed him over to them to be crucified.

So the soldiers took charge of Jesus. Carrying his own cross, he went out to the place of the Skull (which in Aramaic is called Golgotha). There they crucified him, and with him two others—one on each side and Jesus in the middle.

John 19:1-18, NIV

After this, Jesus knowing that all things were now accomplished, that the scripture might be fulfilled, saith, I thirst. Now there was set a vessel full of vinegar: and they filled a spunge with vinegar, and put it upon hyssop, and put it to his mouth. When Jesus therefore had received the vinegar, he said, It is finished: and he bowed his head, and gave up the ghost.

John 19:28-30, KJV

Jesus could have called 10,000 angels to come to His rescue from the abusive crowd, to avoid the suffering He experienced while hanging nailed to that cross for hours—but He did not. He chose to remain there, knowing that He was the only way—the Lamb without blemish—for each of us to be restored to a two-way relationship with Father God. As He hung there, in the place of you and I, "At noon, darkness came over the whole land until three in the afternoon. And at three in the afternoon Jesus cried out in a loud voice, 'Eloi, Eloi, lama sabachthani?' (Which means 'My God, my God, why have you forsaken me?')" (Mark 15:33-34, NIV). At this moment, Jesus sensed that He was utterly forsaken by God, representing the brokenness between God and man. "But your iniquities have separated you from your God; your sins have hidden his face from you, so that he will not hear" (Isaiah 59:2, NIV).

And what happened next is what differentiates God from any other god or prophet that others may choose to follow.

> For even if there are so-called gods, whether in heaven or on earth (as indeed there are many "gods" and many "lords"), yet for us there is but one God, the Father, from whom all things came and for whom we live; and there is but one Lord, Jesus Christ, through whom all things came and through whom we live.
>
> 1 Corinthians 8:5-6, NIV

Just as much as the broken relationship applies to each of us, so does the victory over death and the restoration of a two-way relationship with our Heavenly Father. "Looking unto Jesus the author and finisher of our faith; who for the joy that was set before him endured the cross, despising the shame, and is set down at the right hand of the throne of God" (Hebrews 12:2, KJV).

After three days, Jesus rose out of the tomb and returned to Heaven to be restored in His full glory at the right hand of the throne of God. Jesus conquered death! He is alive and reachable and waiting to hear from each one of us! No other god or prophet has escaped the power of death's grip nor holds the power to restore any of us to a relationship with Almighty God. "The Son is the radiance of God's glory and the exact representation of his being, sustaining all things by his powerful word. After he had provided purification for sins, he sat down at the right hand of the Majesty in heaven" (Hebrews 1:3, NIV).

Let this mind be in you, which was also in Christ Jesus: Who, being in the form of God, thought it not robbery to be equal with God: But made himself of no reputation, and took upon him the form of a servant, and was made in the likeness of men: And being found in fashion as a man, he humbled himself, and became obedient unto death, even the death of the cross. Wherefore God also hath highly exalted him, and given him a name which is above every name: That at the name of Jesus every knee should bow, of things in heaven, and things in earth, and things under the earth; And that every tongue should confess that Jesus Christ is Lord, to the glory of God the Father.

Philippians 2:5-11, KJV

The fulfillment of God's restoration plan was through Jesus. Without Jesus, there is no victory over death nor restoration of our relationship with God the Father. He reveals this plan to all who will open their hearts and hear His loving Spirit whispering to draw near to Him.

And all these things that men have told over and over for generations have come true. The greatest of all these truths is that God loved us enough that He would have His Son be born as a human being to live and grow up as each of us do. Even today, people all over the world continue to celebrate this one baby boy's birth: Jesus, the Son of Creator God. And all of nature which He created exclaims His glory!

But wait—Jesus, the Son of God, born of a virgin? To many, it sounds much like a fairy tale! Our Creator

God understood how our human minds would try to reason with His birth so much that He created woman to bear babies as a witness that miracles do happen! I am still amazed that my human body carried life inside of me, created in the image of God; and even now as I write this book, my daughter who I birthed, is now carrying life and preparing to give birth to yet another life. Think about this. Each little one is a miracle—how can this be? Whether we understand the *how*, each life *is!* We may not understand *how* Jesus was born of a virgin and existed as a man before conquering death, but He *is!* Do not allow your human mind to limit God's reality in your life.

No matter what we say, do, or believe, it does not change who God is or the fact that He is the one true and alive God, Creator of the world. "Jesus Christ is the same yesterday and today and forever" (Hebrews 13:8, NIV).

In God's time, Jesus began to reach those who would listen and reach out to Him in faith. As a child, I listened to the words of God's love, and with child-like faith, I believed. Now, as an adult, I can't help but understand how hearing these words for the first time a person might think it sounds like a fairy tale. From what I'm about to share, it will soon become clear that once I trusted in child-like faith, my experiences convinced me that God's Word is truth. Just as a baby first learns to take small steps, grow in the trust to take larger steps, and then eventually run, I, too, had to take baby steps of faith before I had the confidence to take the larger steps. With each step of faith I took, I began to experience the truth of God's grace and love. I have now gained confidence that I can run the course with joy because of the trust I have gained in my Father God. Even when I still fail because of my human nature, I have confidence that my Abba Father sees me, not as a failure, but as I will be once I pass through the gates of heaven and into His presence.

In each of the following chapters (not to worry, most are short!), I will share experiences where God showed Himself to be real and present, which brought me to the point of full belief and trust in Him. This is my journey...

# Protection in Time of Need...*Angels Abound*

As I approached my twenties, I wanted to exercise my independence and strike out on my own. I decided to move to the big city of Grand Rapids, Michigan. Anyone familiar with this city knows that the famous 28th Street is one of the busiest during rush hour traffic. I had just picked up my car from the service garage and turned off of 28th Street onto Hwy U.S. 31. It was definitely another very busy road during rush hour! The unfortunate happened and my car began to stall. Alone in a big city, I began to realize that I was miles from my apartment and had no one to call. It didn't matter anyway since this was "pre-cell phone" days and there was no payphone on the side of the highway. Panic should have set in, don't you think?

I was able to pull off on the side of the highway just in time as the car completely conked out. (Yes, that is a mechanical term in case anyone is wondering.) As I got out of my car and proceeded to open the hood, a car full of young—shall I say "undesirables"—slowed down next to me. Did they offer to get out and help? No, instead they shouted, "Hey, baby, looks like mama needs a ride. Come on and hop in with us."

My response? "Uh, no thank you...help is already on the way." Truthfully, I knew help was on the way; I just didn't know from where yet.

Previously, I said I had no one to call...that wasn't exactly true. I got back in my car and made a call to heaven. His phone line is always open. "God, you know I'm in a situation down here. It is getting dark, and this is not the safest place to be. I know you didn't send that car of questionable characters. So, Lord, I am praying and trusting that the next car that stops will be sent by you. Amen."

Within minutes, another car stopped beside me, and that driver asked if there was anything he could do to help. My response this time, "Yes, if you could give me a ride, I would appreciate it. But if you try anything, I can make you hurt really bad." I said this with a smile, of course, with a hope that he would believe that this young girl could actually hurt him! To this day, I can still hear Jim's chuckle and picture his grin as he said, "Understood, no worries."

As we drove away, Jim asked me where he could give me a ride to. As I explained where I lived, and that I didn't expect him to drive me all that way (over fifteen miles), he turned and looked at me as he said nonchalantly, "No problem, my wife and I live in that same apartment complex." Not only did they live in the same complex, but it was also in the building next to mine! It turned out that Jim also worked in the plant where I worked in an office in downtown Grand Rapids, and I wrote out his payroll check! (Yes, I meant "wrote out," things were done manually then. Am I dating myself?)

It gets better...I later discovered that he and his wife were from my hometown area from which I had recently moved! Coincidence? If I had not prayed specifically and placed my situation in God's hands, it could be labeled coincidence. I did pray, however, and placed my trust in Him—God heard my prayer and answered with more proof than I could even imagine. God is real and reachable at any time.

The question is: Do *we* call on *Him*? Is our trust and walk with *Him* real?

> The LORD is my rock, my fortress and my
> deliverer; my God is my rock, in whom I take

refuge, my shield and the horn of my salvation, my stronghold.

Psalm 18:2, NIV

# Falling Star...*God Answers Knee Mail*

One evening after reading some Scriptures, I knelt by the side of my bed and entered a special time of prayer with God. Many times, we come to Him with requests before we even thank Him for who He is and for His unconditional love for us. In this prayer time, I made it a point to come before Him thanking Him for all that He had been to me; for being there for me through all the good times and bad, and for loving me for who I was at that time knowing what I would become by following Him...all before I prayed and asked Him for anything.

I was also conscious of the fact that many times we spend so much time talking during our prayer time that God does not have a chance to speak to our hearts through His Holy Spirit (a conversation involves two being allowed to speak; not just one doing the talking and one doing the listening). "But they that wait upon the Lord shall renew their strength; they shall mount up with wings as eagles; they shall run, and not be weary; and they shall walk, and not faint" (Isaiah 40:31, KJV). One of my favorite old hymns we used to sing in church ended this scripture with, "Teach me, Lord, teach me, Lord, to wait."

I waited on Him and experienced such a sweet peace that when I stood up and opened my eyes, I knew I had touched the throne of God. I moved to the window and, with eyes filled with tears, gazed out upon the night sky filled with stars.

I thought about how Creator God had caused the shadow on the sundial to go backward ten degrees as a sign to Hezekiah. We read this account in Isaiah 38.

In those days was Hezekiah sick unto death. And Isaiah the prophet the son of Amoz came unto him, and said unto him, Thus saith the Lord, Set thine house in order: for thou shalt die, and not live.

Then Hezekiah turned his face toward the wall, and prayed unto the Lord, And said, Remember now, O Lord, I beseech thee, how I have walked before thee in truth and with a perfect heart, and have done that which is good in thy sight. And Hezekiah wept sore.

Then came the word of the Lord to Isaiah, saying, Go, and say to Hezekiah, Thus saith the Lord, the God of David thy father, I have heard thy prayer, I have seen thy tears: behold, I will add unto thy days fifteen years. And I will deliver thee and this city out of the hand of the king of Assyria: and I will defend this city. And this shall be a sign unto thee from the Lord, that the Lord will do this thing that he hath spoken; Behold, I will bring again the shadow of the degrees, which is gone down in the sun dial of Ahaz, ten degrees backward. So the sun returned ten degrees, by which degrees it was gone down.

Isaiah 38:1-8, KJV

Remembering this scripture, I knew with confidence that the very God I had just spent time with had placed every one of those stars as well as all the planets, sun, and moon into place.

Knowing what a special time it had been for me in prayer, somehow, I wanted a confirmation that it had been just as special to God. As I gazed out on those stars, I could not recall ever seeing a falling star and thought this could be something I could ask God for as a confirmation; to see a falling star in just that exact area of the night sky I was looking at.

As quickly as this thought entered my mind—just as quick—I heard the voice of the enemy whispering to me that if I wanted to see a falling star, I would have to look in other parts of the sky. I immediately rebuked this thought and told the enemy to "get lost" because my God was bigger than even my human mind could ever imagine—that He is the one who placed every star in the sky and would answer my request in the very part of the sky that my eyes were not veering from. In those very seconds that followed, there before my eyes was a beautiful falling star! My inner spirit quickened knowing I served an alive God whose glory is revealed in the heavens above and that if I kept my eyes on Him just as I kept my eyes from veering from a specific part of the sky, I would see His glory in His fullness!

As we enter into our prayer at the feet of His throne, we must let go of our thoughts and desires, and withdraw ourselves from all that which would distract us from hearing the voice of our Abba Father. As we wait upon God, He will reveal Himself to us. As we surrender and become a broken vessel before Him, He will pour Himself into us and His love will fall upon us. This is where our spirit comes into communion with God's

Holy Spirit. He is waiting on us and this is where we find Him in His fullness. His answers to our prayers will be manifested in a way that others will see His realness and also draw closer to Him.

We are also to bring our needs to Him with the same heart and assurance as we do our praise and thankfulness for His presence in our lives. Once we bring a need before the throne of God, we need to leave it there in faith, trusting He will answer with the best answer. In those times our heart is so heavy that no human words can express what we want to communicate regarding the need, we can trust the Holy Spirit to step in and carry our heartfelt thoughts to Jesus. God provides us His Holy Spirit because He knows we need His presence, His added strength, to survive in this imperfect world.

Ask with the assurance that God will supply. "But my God shall supply all your need according to His riches in glory by Christ Jesus" (Philippians 4:19, KJV). We ask in faith and then wait in anticipation for His answer.

> For in this hope we were saved. But hope that is seen is no hope at all. Who hopes for what they already have? But if we hope for what we do not yet have, we wait for it patiently. In the same way, the Spirit helps us in our weakness. We do not know what we

ought to pray for, but the Spirit himself intercedes for us through wordless groans.

Romans 8:24-26, NIV

When we pray, our faith is in our Heavenly Father, for what other god or prophet has His power? The Lord himself demonstrated just who He is in His powerful response to Job.

Then the Lord spoke to Job out of the storm. He said:

"Who is this that obscures my plans with words without knowledge? Brace yourself like a man; I will question you, and you shall answer me.

"Where were you when I laid the earth's foundation? Tell me, if you understand. Who marked off its dimensions? Surely you know! Who stretched a measuring line across it? On what were its footings set, or who laid its cornerstone—while the morning stars sang together and all the angels shouted for joy?

"Who shut up the sea behind doors when it burst forth from the womb, when I made the clouds its garment and wrapped it in thick darkness, when I fixed limits for it and set its doors and bars in place, when I said, 'This far you may come and no farther; here is where your proud waves halt'?

"Have you ever given orders to the morning, or shown the dawn its place, that it might take the earth by the edges and shake the wicked out of it? The earth takes shape like clay under a seal; its features stand out like those of a garment. The wicked are denied their light, and their upraised arm is broken.

"Have you journeyed to the springs of the sea or walked in the recesses of the deep? Have the gates of death been shown to you? Have you seen the gates of the deepest darkness? Have you comprehended the vast expanses of the earth? Tell me, if you know all this.

"What is the way to the abode of light? And where does darkness reside? Can you take them to their places? Do you know the paths to their dwellings? Surely you know, for you were already born! You have lived so many years!

"Have you entered the storehouses of the snow or seen the storehouses of the hail, which I reserve for times of trouble, for days of war and battle? What is the way to the place where the lightning is dispersed, or the place where the east winds are scattered over the earth? Who cuts a channel for the torrents of rain, and a path for the thunderstorm, to water a land where no one lives, an uninhabited desert, to satisfy a desolate wasteland and make it sprout with grass? Does the rain have a father? Who fathers the drops of dew? From whose womb comes the ice? Who gives birth to the frost from the heavens when the waters become hard as stone, when the surface of the deep is frozen?

"Can you bind the chains of the Pleiades? Can you loosen Orion's belt? Can you bring forth the constellations in their seasons or lead out the Bear with its cubs? Do you know the laws of the heavens? Can you set up God's dominion over the earth?

"Can you raise your voice to the clouds and cover yourself with a flood of water? Do you send the lightning bolts on their way? Do they report to you, 'Here we are'? Who gives the ibis wisdom or gives the rooster understanding? Who has the wisdom to count the clouds? Who can tip over the water jars of the heavens when the dust becomes hard and the clods of earth stick together?

"Do you hunt the prey for the lioness and satisfy the hunger of the lions when they crouch in their dens or lie in wait in a thicket? Who provides food for the raven when its young cry out to God and wander about for lack of food?"

Job 38, NIV

God continued His conversation with Job as He pointed out His greatness and ended with, "Will the one who contends with the Almighty correct him? Let him who accuses God answer him!" (Job 40:2, NIV).

Praise Him, prayerfully leave your needs at the feet of this amazing Father God, and then trust!

Clap your hands, all you nations; shout to God with cries of joy. For the Lord Most High is awesome, the great King over all the earth. He subdued nations under us, peoples under our feet. He chose our inheritance for us, the pride of Jacob, whom he loved. God has ascended amid shouts of joy, the Lord amid the sounding of trumpets. Sing praises to God, sing praises; sing praises to our King, sing praises. For God is the King of all the earth; sing to him a psalm of praise. God reigns over the nations; God is seated on his holy throne. The nobles of the nations assemble as the people of the God of Abraham, for the kings of the earth belong to God; he is greatly exalted.

Psalm 47, NIV

# 3

# Holding Hands...
## *In Training by the Holy Spirit*

It doesn't matter whether we are the simplest thinkers in the world, or the smartest, God's message is simple enough for each of us to grasp and for good reason. Even the smartest person will find themselves in situations of confusion or distraction where only the simplest message will penetrate the mind, make sense, and provide answers. As in the example in the previous chapter, the enemy does not want us to hear God's voice. He mimics God's voice and interjects his lies to trip us up. This is why it is so important to allow the Holy Spirit to "train" us to recognize the difference between God's truths and the enemy's lies. We need to continually be "in training". God is an awesome teacher and has provided a powerful source of wisdom through His Holy Spirit. Paul wrote:

And I, brethren, when I came to you, came not with excellency of speech or of wisdom, declaring unto you the testimony of God. For I determined not to know any thing among you, save Jesus Christ, and him crucified. And I was with you in weakness, and in fear, and in much trembling. And my speech and my preaching was not with enticing words of man's wisdom, but in demonstration of the Spirit and of power: That your faith should not stand in the wisdom of men, but in the power of God. Howbeit we speak wisdom among them that are perfect: yet not the wisdom of this world, nor of the princes of this world, that come to nought: But we speak the wisdom of God in a mystery, even the hidden wisdom, which God ordained before the world unto our glory: Which none of the princes of this world knew: for had they known it, they would not have crucified the Lord of glory. But as it is written, Eye hath not seen, nor ear heard, neither have entered into the heart of man, the things which God hath prepared for them that love him. But God hath revealed them unto us by his Spirit: for the Spirit searcheth all things, yea, the deep things of God...

Now we have received, not the spirit of the
world, but the spirit which is of God; that we
might know the things that are freely given to
us of God. Which things also we speak, not in
the words which man's wisdom teacheth, but
which the Holy Ghost teacheth; comparing
spiritual things with spiritual.

1 Cor 2:1-10; 12-13, KJV

By recognizing His voice in the simpler experiences,
we are "in training" to distinguish His voice in the more
complicated situations—from the enemy's or even our
self-motivated inner voices.

One of my personal "simpler" experiences came as
I was standing in church one Sunday morning. Singing along with the worship song, I could sense the Holy
Spirit prompting me to take the hands of those on each
side of me as a sign of one-ness in the sweet worship
we were sharing. In my human self, I hesitated—all
kinds of thoughts began to race through my head about
why I shouldn't "disturb" my neighbor's worship time.
As I continued to experience this prompting, I knew
it was from God. As I pretty much grabbed the hands
of those next to me in obedience to God's prompting,
I watched as neighbor took the hand of neighbor...as
hands reached across the aisle to take the hand of an-

other...and pretty soon the church body was holding hands worshipping in one accord. It was a beautiful time of praise with many eyes wet with tears of happiness acknowledging the awesomeness of our Lord. I was so thankful I had been obedient.

But, the training did not end there. Later that day, I returned to church for the evening service. By the time we arrived, the church was so full that we were forced to sit at the very back of the church—I can still see the very spot on the pew today! As the service continued, the pastor gave a wonderful message which spoke to many hearts. As he was bringing the service to an end, I felt a sense of frustration on his part as to how to bring it to a close. He asked everyone to close their eyes and bow their heads but his words just didn't seem to be coming out the way he wanted them to.

Oh, yeah, I was still in training! (Actually, I was feeling more like, "Oh, no!") I felt the Holy Spirit prompting me to do something even more unheard of for me, and probably for most everyone reading this! I was being prompted to step away from my seat, walk up the aisle, and ask the pastor if I could borrow the microphone to say a few words. *What? Me? Oh, Holy Spirit, are you sure? Do what? But it is such a long way up that aisle! Okay, okay, I will step away from my seat trusting you...but if I get up there and this is not of you, then I am depending on you to shove me to my knees at the altar and you just take it from there!* So, in training, I stepped away from the security of my seat and began walking down the aisle, still trusting God to give me something to say if the pastor granted my request of handing me the microphone.

The reason I said that I still remember the exact place we sat that night is that I distinctly remember just how far away from the front of the church that pew was. The aisle was even longer that evening for some strange reason. I have to admit that I decided to walk up the side aisle rather than the middle so it wouldn't be as noticeable if God directed me to just duck into another pew on the way up and save myself the embarrassment. I was keeping all my options open!

There was no such direction. I arrived at the front of the church and looked straight into the face of the pastor. As I looked at him and he looked at me with a look of confusion, I asked him if I could say a few words. *His* reaction was as though the microphone was a "hot potato" which he hastily handed over to me. *My* immediate reaction was yet another earnest prayer. "Okay, Lord, give me the words to say...*please?*"

As I turned and faced the church with their eyes closed and their heads bowed reverently waiting, God gave me words to share from my heart that touched the hearts of those listening. One by one, they began to also come down to the front of the church and kneel in front of the altar with tears streaming down their faces. God was given the freedom to move over His people as we were obedient to His Spirit speaking to our hearts. He, once again, showed me that His Holy Spirit is real and ever-present and that it is up to us to be continually available to *Him*. The Holy Spirit directs, we speak, and others are blessed.

The church body was blessed by both of these events that day, but that was still not the end of my "training". By both of these events, I saw the results of what can happen when we learn to recognize God's voice and obediently act. God was preparing me in simpler situations for a larger "mission".

The following Sunday, I was at church with my two young children. My husband was out of town on business. All present were in our different Sunday school classes held the hour before the Sunday morning service. I had previously made plans to stop by a friend's church at noon after the Sunday worship service to drop something off for her.

During the Sunday school hour, I felt the Holy Spirit prompting me to leave and go over to my friend's church in between Sunday school class and the worship service. I quickly remembered my "in training" events from the previous Sunday and knew immediately that

I needed to follow this prompting. I went to my parents and asked them to take care of my children until I returned.

As I drove across town, I prayed that God would lead the way for His purpose. When I arrived, I walked into the church lobby and asked someone to locate my friend. A few minutes later, she approached me with a shocked look on her face and asked what I was doing there at that time rather than after church. I just looked at her and told her maybe she could tell me!

She grabbed my arm and started leading me toward a room where the church elders were preparing to meet while explaining how it had to have been God that brought me there at that time. The previous Friday night, the pastor had been at a Bible study group when a woman from the church approached him in front of everyone and told him that she had a word from God for him. She told him that he was to kneel before her while she read her letter. Yes, weird and not how God operates! Thankfully, the pastor had enough wisdom to not kneel before her as requested. This woman, however, continued to read her letter to the pastor and all those present. Needless to say, the letter was highly accusatorial.

The elders were meeting that morning between their Sunday school and worship service to discuss and vote whether to support the accusations presented in this woman's letter or to support the pastor. God wasn't taken by surprise by this situation; He was fully aware of what was transpiring. As the Almighty God so wonderfully does, He had already prepared the way for the truth to be brought to light in this situation.

My friend walked me into the room where the elders were and introduced me as someone who could speak to the character of the pastor's accuser. We began the meeting with prayer, and I told them I would speak only to the facts as I knew them and would not provide an opinion. In just the previous month, I had dealt with this woman and it was discovered that she was stealing money from her customers and misrepresenting sales to her employer. Once the light was shed on what had been discovered about this woman's ungodly character, I left and drove back to my church.

I found out later that the elders had been leaning toward voting against the pastor based on the letter being written in a way that mimicked something that would come from God and sounded like it held the truth. As a result of them hearing the truth about the source of the letter, they voted against the woman and in favor of the pastor. The woman was eventually asked to leave the church.

Many lessons can be learned from this experience. First, God does not expect us to go into battle without His presence and direction. We recognize His presence by reading His Word, becoming familiar with His ways, and allowing Him to train us to recognize His voice. As we are obedient to His prompting, His Holy Spirit guides and directs us. Second, the enemy imitates God's truth to trick us into thinking we are following God's direction. Again, this is why it is important to learn to differentiate His voice from the enemy's or our own will. Third, the enemy hates anything of God and wants to destroy from within. This can be by attacking a pastor to destroy the church, a family by destroying it through a divorce, or a country by deceiving the citizens with his lies discounting the realness of God's love and grace. Stay aware.

Be assured. Our faithful God is with us in all things, He is real, like no other god or prophet. And when He sends us on a "mission", He leads the way. Annais is a great example.

In Damascus there was a disciple named Ananias. The Lord called to him in a vision, "Ananias!" "Yes, Lord," he answered. The Lord told him, "Go to the house of Judas on Straight Street and ask for a man from Tarsus named

Saul, for he is praying. In a vision he has seen a man named Ananias come and place his hands on him to restore his sight." "Lord," Ananias answered, "I have heard many reports about this man and all the harm he has done to your holy people in Jerusalem. And he has come here with authority from the chief priests to arrest all who call on your name."

But the Lord said to Ananias, "Go! This man is my chosen instrument to proclaim my name to the Gentiles and their kings and to the people of Israel. I will show him how much he must suffer for my name."

Then Ananias went to the house and entered it. Placing his hands on Saul, he said, "Brother Saul, the Lord—Jesus, who appeared to you on the road as you were coming here—has sent me so that you may see again and be filled with the Holy Spirit." Immediately, something like scales fell from Saul's eyes, and he could see again. He got up and was baptized, and after taking some food, he regained his strength.

Acts 9:10-19, NIV

I'm sure God understood Annais' concern; after all, Saul was the most feared persecutor of God's faithful followers. I know I would have done a bit of debating of my own! What if Annais had not recognized God's voice? What if he had not trusted God's direction and followed through? Saul, whose dual name was Paul, became a very influential minister to many during his life. Are we learning to recognize God's voice and following His direction in our walk with Him?

The negative impact of allowing ourselves to listen to the enemy's voice, or that of another created human being, rather than God's is great. The *positive* impact on our lives offers great rewards when we listen to the voice of the Creator who understands exactly who and where each one of us is. Go back and read that again. And again. And again.

# 4

# As the Deer Pants for Streams of Water...*Aware of God's Presence and Truths*

At another point in my life, I was struggling with a few things where I really couldn't see the answers clearly. It was springtime in northern Michigan when the snow was melting and green grass was just starting to grow in the patches of visible, bare ground. At the back of our property were a few of these spots where the deer would come to graze after a long winter. God knew how important these graceful creatures had become to me as a result of a Ladies Retreat I had held in our home with a theme from Psalm 42:1, "As the deer pants for streams of water, so my soul pants for you, my God" (NIV). These words continue to speak to my heart—He is my heart's desire; whether in a valley or on a mountaintop, my soul thirsts for Him.

As I stood at the kitchen window gazing out over the field, my experience with the falling star came to mind. I thought to myself, *I could ask God to show me a deer as confirmation.* He was guiding me during this time of struggle. Then I thought to myself, *Now, why would I do that when I already know that God is with me as a result of all the other ways He has shown me?* I decided I would not ask God so that I could exercise my faith, but show Him that I trusted in my relationship with Him; that I knew He was going through this difficult time with me.

I completely let go of the thought of asking for a deer to appear and finished my breakfast. I then went back upstairs and began to get ready for the day. As I walked by a window, I quickly glanced out to the back of the house, and what do you think I saw? Absolutely! A doe and fawn came leaping right up to the back of our house underneath that very window. They explored around for a few short minutes and then bounded out of sight as quickly as they came. If I hadn't glanced out the window right at that time, I would have missed them!

Was that a coincidence? Many deer have been seen in the field over the years but to have those two come leaping up at that very exact time? What do you think? God is present in so many situations in our lives, but we don't look for Him. In missing the opportunity to recognize Him, we miss the opportunity to see just how real He is and also His faithfulness to reveal Himself to us. With each step that we acknowledge His presence, our faith in Him grows and our two-way relationship becomes stronger.

Yet with all these experiences seeing God in His fullness, there are still times I ask myself how I can believe in this "being" that I've never seen with my own eyes and who sounds like a "fairy tale."

Looking to His Word for answers to our questions of His realness, we find that in Mark 9, Jesus has just told a desperate father that his son can be healed if he believes. The father responds in honesty, "I do believe; help me overcome my unbelief!" (Mark 9:24, NIV). The father's response laid his faith alongside his doubt and fear. He was honest with Jesus and to himself. What did Jesus do? He did not turn his back because of the doubt and fear the father voiced. Instead, He delivered the man's son and healed him.

Questioning is not a bad thing—it is actually a good thing when we are honest with ourselves and with God. He already knows our hearts and thoughts. It is in questioning that we come to a place of answers. The answer to my questions always returns to the way God has revealed Himself in so many ways that there can be no other explanation. And then I rejoice knowing, *in faith*, that He loves me enough that He brings me along from baby steps to even bigger steps in my faith in Jesus Christ, the Son of God—the only one who has ever walked away from an empty tomb and reclaimed His glory in heaven. There are no other gods, no other prophets, no other world leaders who have or can accomplish what God has. God is the beginning and the end. He is the Creator of all. When we can have the fullest of blessings from our Creator God, why would anyone choose to serve and honor and believe in a created person, nature, or idol? It just does not make sense.

*5*

# In the Face of Adversity...*Staying in the Will of God*

Can we all agree that "life happens"? We can have the best-laid plans and the best intentions, but life throws us curve balls that are out of our control. My husband, Bob, and I were probably one of the last couples that anyone expected to file for a divorce. I never saw us as being divorced. Uh, oh, the big "D" word...yikes! Without sharing the details of "why", it is enough to say that we were dealing with some issues that not many outside the four walls of our home could see. Unfortunately, our son and daughter could see and were being affected by it. I knew that the only way to break the negativity in our home was for either Bob or I to leave the household, however, I also did not want to be out of the will of God in getting a divorce.

For months, I prayed and searched the Scriptures. In one of my quiet moments, I read 1 Corinthians 7:10-11, "Now to the married I command, yet not I but the Lord: A wife is not to depart from her husband. But even if she does depart, let her remain unmarried or be reconciled to her husband. And a husband is not to divorce his wife" (NKJV). So, I prayed that if God provided me the name of a divorce attorney somehow, someway, on that day, under the circumstances, that would be my confirmation He was releasing me from the marriage. Included in my prayer was that I would stay available to a reconciliation if that should happen in the future. If I didn't receive the name of an attorney, I would remain at home and continue to pray that things would change.

I left for work that day as usual. My office was a little closet-size room that had been turned into an office with no windows, not even in the door. I was pretty much shut off from the world, just me and my computer. How did I expect God to provide me the name of a divorce attorney? It would have to be a God thing.

That afternoon, I heard a knock on the door, and a health department nurse stuck her head in the door to say hi. Our conversation continued beyond the hello, so she came in and sat down for a few minutes to visit. During that short conversation, you guessed it, I can't remember why, but the name of the attorney who had handled her divorce came up. The lights went on inside my head at that moment, and I thought about how ever-present and caring my God is.

I did file for divorce, all the while remembering my commitment to stay available to future reconciliation. I am happy to say that a few years later, by God's hand, Bob and I reconciled and we are better friends than ever. We both came to a place that we admitted we had been immature and selfish, taking each other for granted. We've learned a lot and come a long way since that storm in our lives. God answered my prayer but already had a plan where He would bring us back together again, despite ourselves!

I don't share this event in my life in the judgment of others who have gone through a divorce—there are many reasons why this can happen. I only share to tell of the lesson I learned; no matter the storm, we need to stay available to God's plan for our lives. Our family and friends may judge us, the church may judge us—it does not matter. What does matter is that we remain in the will of our Heavenly Father according to His Word. He will bring healing where it is needed. It may be on this earth or in heaven. He will bring purpose where it is needed, according to His plan. He will bring understanding where it is needed, through His Holy Spirit.

He will provide finances where it is needed; His storehouses are full, just trust Him. He will bring whatever answer is needed. It is for us to lay our need at the foot of His throne, believe in faith that He is real and reachable, and wait for His perfect answer in His perfect time whatever the storm.

I've had people ask me, "How can we be sure the 'answer' is from God and not just our own will?" We need to dig into His Word and confirm that what we think is His answer aligns with Scripture. He has provided His Word as a way to communicate His truths to us.

Is the Bible always easy to understand? It is for us to pray and ask for understanding. It is that part of God, the Holy Spirit, which helps us to understand God's truths. "But the Comforter, which is the Holy Ghost, whom the Father will send in my name, he shall teach you all things, and bring all things to your remembrance, whatsoever I have said unto you" (John 14:26, KJV).

Sure, there are still parts of the Bible I do not understand. I hope that God will schedule quite a bit of time for me once I get to heaven because I am still going to have *a lot* of questions. His basic truths, however, are very easily understood and that is what we need to stay focused on—how to grow in our relationship with our Creator God, our Heavenly Father.

# 6

# Going Where I've Never Been Before...*Making it Through the "Desert"*

During the time I was divorced, I was in my living room one afternoon, enjoying a time of worship with some wonderful Christian music playing in the background. I was at that time and am even more so now, in awe of the splendor of my loving, Heavenly Father. As I was worshipping, I was also praying and asking God, once again, for the direction I should take over the next few months. I knew where I was at in life was just a stepping stone to the next stage of what God had for me.

Previously, I felt like the near future would involve a move to another town, but I just didn't know where. I thought about moving to Phoenix, Arizona to be closer to my brother and his children but had emphatically ruled that hot desert out as any possibility. I had even taken a long trip from Michigan to Tennessee, stopping and exploring many areas along the way, to see if I felt a nudge from God showing me where I was to move. I returned home with no "nudges".

I continued to pray about it, not even realizing all the while, I was setting perimeters on it based on my desires. I had already ruled out Arizona and I also wanted to be close enough to get back to Michigan in a reasonable day's drive. Hmm...how did that work out for me giving God perimeters? I'm being honest and human here, folks. God cares about our desires but we cannot tie His hands because of them. By doing so, we can miss both important lessons and blessings. God definitely has a sense of humor; keep reading, and you'll see what I mean!

As I continued to worship that afternoon, and as I was expressing to God that I wanted to know more of Him, I heard His Spirit gently whisper, "Do you mean it? Do you really mean it when you say you want to go deeper with Jesus?" Okay, I was being called out! And by God's Spirit, no less! I responded with all of my being, "Oh, yes, I want to experience more of God!" I felt God's Spirit wash over me and whisper, "Then you are going into unfamiliar territory." At that point, I had no clue what that meant...this began my journey of the next two years in my "desert" coming face to face with myself and with God.

Within the week of hearing that I would be going into unfamiliar territory and not having a clue what that meant, I received a phone call that provided my direction. Earlier in the day, I felt like I should call my brother who lived in Phoenix, but I put it off. Within an hour of this nudge (that I did not listen to! I also am human!) I received a phone call, and it was my brother who very, very rarely called me. I asked him, "What are you calling me for? I was thinking of calling you!" The conversation quickly turned to discussing the possibilities of me moving to Arizona. Remember, this was not in the areas I had visited on my trip, was definitely not within a day's drive back to Michigan, and it was a hot desert I had said I would not move to! By the end of that phone call, I heard myself making plans for me to move to Phoenix!

Once I hung up, I asked myself, "What did I just agree to?" The amazing thing was that I had such a peace knowing it was the direction I was to go. I was moving in faith—literally!

I was there within a month of that phone call. I admit that it happened so fast and in faith that I didn't even give it a thought that I was moving to a very large city that was the capital of Arizona. As evidence, on the drive down, we stopped for lunch after driving through a large city with freeways crisscrossing through it. I casually asked my brother (he flew up to Michigan and drove my U-Haul down to AZ), "I won't be having to deal with large highways like this in Phoenix, will I?"

He just looked at me dumbfounded and laughed while responding, "Hello...the city of Phoenix has nothing *but!*" It didn't take me long to realize this, but hey, I was getting out of the snow of northern Michigan winters, right? I could do this!

As we drove closer to Phoenix, we passed through a town to the north, high in elevation. I had just left a snowstorm in Michigan, driven across the country on dry ground, and what do you think we ran into? A snowstorm and icy roads in the town of Flagstaff. I asked myself, "What have I gotten myself into? Freeways and more snow!"

The drive down the mountain that night provided me the definition of "fear and trembling". All the other drivers were driving like they were familiar with the road and were flying down the mountainside even though the roads were icy. As semis flew around the curves, I could see their trailers leaning as if they would go over the edge at any time. The slush that the other vehicles threw up from their tires immediately covered my headlights and dimmed them. In the darkness of the night and not knowing the road, this was not good. My brother, who was driving the U-Haul somewhere ahead of me, called me on my cell phone and asked me if I was still behind him. I responded, "Can you see my flashers?" When he answered, "No," in my anxiousness, I yelled at the equally-tired guy, "Then I am not behind you!" and immediately broke down in tears. I was alone on that dark, icy, unfamiliar, very steep mountainside. This night began my true "desert" experience. I was completely dependent on God to get me safely through to my destination. I realized then that my destination was not "Phoenix", but it was the "unfamiliar territory" that only God would bring me through.

I made it down that mountain. At midnight, my brother, nephews, and nieces unpacked my U-Haul, assembled my bed, and left, leaving me alone and extremely tired. I cried...and then cried some more. I cried many more tears many more nights, but never once did I ask God to take me back to where I had come from because I knew, without a shadow of a doubt, that I was where I was supposed to be.

God blessed me in so many ways as I was getting settled in the northwest part of Phoenix. As a Realtor, my niece had found me a rental in a good neighborhood. I found a church that I grew to love, and joined a Meetup group where we enjoyed many fun times out; I made life-long friends who I cherish still today. There were so many good memories experienced among what I'm about to share.

It didn't take long to realize what God meant by "unfamiliar territory". I realized I had been willing to take this "leap of faith" because I knew I was going to have the help of my brother to start my own business, and that I also had $6,000 cash to get me through until my business would start generating income. Read that again...my "faith" was in that I had enough cash to hold me through until my business started generating income. Being honest with myself, I questioned whether, if I had not had that cash or the thought of my brother helping me start my own business, would I have had faith enough in God to make that long, cross-country move?

It hit me that finances would be my "desert". I had never had to worry about money. I began working at an early age and always had good jobs that paid well. When I was married, we had a good income and lived comfortably—not extravagantly, but comfortably. I knew that I had lost sight of where I placed my faith. If all my money was completely stripped away, would I *still* trust in my Lord as I claimed I did?

I cried myself to sleep many nights. I was crying because of the realization of the lesson God had for me. It was going to be a tough one, but I never grumbled against God or blamed Him. I knew that Arizona was literally a desert but it was to be my "desert" just like the Israelite's desert. I would wander around that desert for enough years until I finally learned the lessons God had for me. My prayer was that I wouldn't miss the lesson and that I would see the depth of God's provision through it all. Although I cried, I trusted that God would go through the tough times with me and bring me out on the other side and that I would know Him in a much fuller way...as well as test my level of faith.

As the months went by, I watched how fast the remaining money slipped through my hands for unforeseen expenses. I experienced my business not succeeding and having to work temp jobs to scrape by living on credit cards. I was paying high monthly rent and utilities, payments on two hospital stays and other health expenses, four major car repairs—being forced to sell my already-paid-for "lemon" and going into debt for another car—and many more unforeseen expenses. Again, I cried and cried but never grumbled. I knew that God's purpose was for me to have everything stripped away and me in a place I had never been so that I was totally dependent upon Him.

Somewhere in the middle of all of this, I finally land-
ed a position at a company that I enjoyed very much. Although the pay was reasonable and my co-workers were
great, my finances were not...I was still living partially
on credit cards because of the cost of living in the area.
I continued to cry to God at night but held on in anticipation of His answer which I knew would surely come.
I confess that, through those trials, it crossed my mind
more than once that I probably had incurred enough
debt that I could most likely qualify for bankruptcy. I
don't judge those who have taken this path because I
have not walked in their shoes, but I knew that it wasn't
the right answer for me. This was a legitimate debt that
had sustained me while going through this "desert",
and I trusted that God would eventually provide a way
for me to pay it...He was faithful!

It was a sad day when I got the news that my
position at the Arizona company was in jeopardy and
I could be without a job soon. I continued to pray and
trust God as my faith continued to grow. Opportunities
arose for different positions in the Phoenix area that
looked like an obvious solution to my income situation,
however, as I've learned many times, the most obvious
is not always God's answer. I waited for His plan.

Bob (yes, divorced but friends) called and said the
company he was working for might be looking for an-

other person and that he had recommended me. We discussed the day rate that I should ask for if they, indeed, called and offered me an opportunity to work on the same project as Bob. After hanging up, I prayed about this possibility that would mean leaving Arizona and moving to the opposite side of the country to Pennsylvania. I wanted to be sure that it was God's plan for me and not something that could materialize just because of the project needing another hard worker.

So, I prayed that if it was God's will for me, this contract company would accept my day rate at an even higher one than what Bob and I had discussed. I wanted this to be a "God-thing". The phone call came, and in the end, my increased day rate was accepted, and I knew it was from God. In just under three weeks, I gave my notice, had a ginormous garage sale, packed my remaining items, and had them moved to a storage unit, sold my car, canceled all the utilities, said goodbye to my AZ family and friends, and flew to Pennsylvania. I had such peace that this was the direction God had for me.

What was supposed to be three months of work turned into six-and-a-half years! It was confirmed that this was a "God-thing" and He provided for me to get completely out of the debt I had incurred while in my "desert", as well as many other blessings. I became the

Crew Chief over a great crew of more than fifteen people and found a wonderful, loving church family who I
will always cherish! It was also through this that God
brought Bob and I back together! Since we have been
back together, we have once again been able to help one
another through some challenging times as well as celebrate many special holidays, vacations, and other special memories as a family.

There were so many lessons learned in that desert—
in Arizona—one of the perimeters I had placed on God's
direction for the next stage of my life! The perimeters
we place on what we allow God to do in our lives greatly
affects how He will answer. I appreciate His continued
patience with me as I learn to "let go and let God" in my
life. Look at all I would have missed; hills and valleys
alike have brought me where I am today!

Also proven in this "desert" experience is that God
does not promise us a life of all mountaintop experiences. When we come out on the other side of our "valleys"
we experience and look back, we can see God's presence
through it all—even learn a lesson or two from it. We
realize the truth provided to us in 1 Thessalonians 5:18,
"In every thing give thanks: for this is the will of God in
Christ Jesus concerning you" (KJV).

Were answers provided in my timeframe? No! As
humans, we so often grow impatient and wonder where

God's answer is, but His answers are always perfect and timely. They may not even be the answers we want, but He still proves that He is in control and has a plan. He wants us to allow Him to work in our lives so that our faith in His realness and His reachability becomes ever so real to us.

# 7

# Back Surgery...
# *Taking God Out of the Box*

A few years into working in Pennsylvania, the evidence of many extended hours in front of the computer started taking its toll. I had suffered from periodic back issues for years but had always been able to bounce back with chiropractic treatment and rest. The day I realized I was in deep trouble was the day I strained my back so badly I couldn't bend over far enough to reach into the refrigerator. The only way I was going to eat was to order something to be delivered. I called Bob (who was back in Michigan at the time) and explained to him that I needed him to come to Pennsylvania and drive me back to Michigan. I needed to be treated by the only chiropractor who had been able to help me in the past. Within two days, Bob came to get me, and I ended up laying down in the back seat of the car for the entire trip home in extreme pain.

For the next year-and-a-half, I worked from the bed while endlessly pursuing an answer to get back my quality of life. I thank God that the company I was contracted with, as well as the client I was sub-contracted to, allowed me to work from Michigan during this time. Despite the pain I was experiencing, God used this time to allow me to be home for a few important family situations as well...one being my mother's treatment of stage four cancer. (God is good—I am happy to say that she is a two-time survivor!)

As a solution to my back pain, local doctors offered physical therapy, injections, and the recommendation to have a nerve block inserted into my back. The latter was not even a consideration for me since it would treat a symptom—not the source—as well as affect a function that was working exactly as God had intended!

I continued to pray for direction. During a phone conversation with my son, he shared with me information on a hospital in Germany where athletes traveled to have their surgeries. He emailed me the website, but after reviewing it, I dismissed it as an opportunity I would not be able to afford. Again, I was putting perimeters on God!

A couple of months later, a gentleman we had come to know through work in Pennsylvania called and told us of his friend who had just returned from Germany after having surgery, and suggested I get in touch with him. I called and spoke to both this gentleman and his wife and found out they were extremely pleased with the surgery results and care received from the hospital staff. I asked him for the contact information so I could investigate it. When they emailed me the link to the website—you guessed it—it was the same place my son had told me about. *Okay, God, are you trying to tell me something?*

Through further investigation, I knew I would need $40,000 out of my own pocket to be able to call and schedule a surgery. I continued to pray that God would provide if this was the direction He would have me go. I added up the money I had available to me in my accounts and continued to save toward this goal.

One afternoon, I was in so much pain while laying in bed that I prayed, "Lord, you know that I have saved $20,000 but it will take me forever to come up with the remaining $20,000. I can't take this pain anymore...if surgery in Germany is your answer for me, you are going to have to provide. I give this to you. In your name, Amen." I ended my prayer, left it at the feet of God, and went on with my workday from my bed.

Later that day, Bob (now the cook) indicated that he didn't feel like cooking dinner that night and asked if I thought I could manage to get ready to go to the restaurant at the casino just five minutes up the highway. Knowing that I would not be able to fix anything for myself because I couldn't stand long enough to cook, I agreed to give it a try. I very gently got myself into the car and endured the ride to the restaurant. I sat with a pillow behind my back and tried to enjoy some time out of the house. I made it through dinner, and as we were walking out the door, I stopped Bob and told him that I wasn't ready to go back home and to bed just yet; it had been too long since I had been able to be out and wanted to delay just a bit longer.

I found a slot machine and put some money in. Right away, I hit $600. I cashed it out and put a little money into another machine and hit $1,000! Whoa, I was definitely ahead! So, I told Bob that I was going to take $100 and put it in another machine and play it down and then go home while I was ahead. I had forgotten about the prayer I prayed earlier that afternoon. Do you know what the awesome thing was, though? God hadn't forgotten!

I got seated, as uncomfortable as it was for me, in front of that next machine, put my $100 in and as I was pushing the button, I turned to Bob to tell him some-

thing. As I was looking at him, I noticed he was looking at my machine and his eyes were getting bigger and
bigger. I looked back at my machine just in time to see
everything line up to win—are you ready for this? Yes,
it was $20,000! I started crying like a baby. Bob asked
me if he needed to get me something to drink to calm
me down! I explained to him through my tears that this
wasn't about the money, it was all about my God being on His throne and showing me that He heard my
prayer that afternoon!

I've shared this story with many since and some
have responded, "Surely God doesn't answer by using
a casino!" Really? I'm not an advocate of gambling but I
say this is proof that it is time to take God out of the box
of our finite mind and allow Him to work in any way He
chooses. I've been able to share this story with so many
as a witness to the realness and the reachability of our
Heavenly Father. This answer to prayer allowed me to
schedule my back surgery for November 2017.

This cost would cover everything except Bob's and
my flight to Germany. My care coordinator also advised
me to purchase 3 seats for myself on the return flight so
that I would be able to lay down. All the money I had,
however, was going toward the surgery and other expenses while there, and a single seat on the flights. I
prayed about the trip back and asked for God to take

care of this as He so faithfully had provided the funds to have the surgery. I left it at His throne.

With my trip and surgery coming up, and all the preparation as well as work to wrap up, I had a day that I just had to take some deep breaths and step away from it all to keep from losing it. Do you want to know just how much our Heavenly Father cares about each of His children? He looked down that day and saw me and my need. A dear Christian brother, Shane, who I had the pleasure of working with, thought he was being prompted to call me about a work question. He quickly realized that God's purpose was for him to call and pray with me. I felt so much better after those powerful words he prayed!

But God wasn't done ministering to my heart. Within minutes of hanging up with Shane, my dear friend, Janet, called out of the blue and added that little extra touch of encouraging words I so greatly needed! It was like "frosting on the cake" to God's grace to me that day. God knows my faults but loves me anyway just the way I am. He knows my heart is full of love and adoration for Him and that my heart desires to bring glory to Him so others will understand that His grace is so much deeper than our human minds will ever comprehend.

That day, He showed me yet again, that *His* heart is full of love...for me. I just don't know how I would make it through this life if it were not for Him going before me each day. Another dear friend gave me a plaque when I left Arizona which said, "Don't worry about tomorrow, God is already there!" Oh, how true this is! How real He is! The path won't always be easy, but we must keep our eyes on the big picture. We may get tired, but we must remember what He has done and trust that He will bring us through.

> Trust in the Lord with all your heart and lean not on your own understanding; in all your ways submit to him, and he will make your paths straight.
>
> Proverbs 3:5-6, NIV

> And the God of all grace, who called you to his eternal glory in Christ, after you have suffered a little while, will himself restore you and make you strong, firm and steadfast. To Him be the power for ever and ever.
>
> 1 Peter 5:10-11, NIV

Before I left for Germany, I met my sister, Susan, for lunch. As we were sitting there, God laid it on her heart to give me something I could take into surgery with me to remind me of God's presence. She scrambled around in her purse and found a package with a small blue cloth to clean her glasses. She opened it, and right there in Panera Bread, we held that little blue cloth together as she prayed.

As they wheeled me into surgery, I told no one of the little blue cloth I had hidden under my pillow. But God's amazing confirmation that He was indeed with me is that when I woke up in recovery, someone had found that little blue cloth and had placed it in my hand!

The story doesn't end there. As Bob and I boarded the plane for our return flight, we found our seats...and what do you think we discovered? The three seats next to us on the plane were vacant! I explained to the stewardess that I was recovering from recent surgery and was wondering if the seats were truly unclaimed. She confirmed it and encouraged me to lay down by bringing me a blanket and a pillow. I slept almost the entire trip back across the big pond! And I didn't have to pay a penny for those extra seats! God's provision is not only sufficient; it is abundant when we trust our needs to Him.

Look back at the beginning of this chapter. I prayed for an answer and God provided it through my son sharing it with me. Because of the "hurdle" of cost, I allowed myself to discount it, but God brought it back around to me a second time. He knew my need and provided when I laid it at His feet and left it there. God's presence in all of this continues to build my great trust in His truths and promises. Do we recognize God's hand in our lives and give Him the credit due to Him? Do we live like we are a child of God? God is a big God... how big is our faith that He is real? Do we *really* believe?

Then Jesus said, "Did I not tell you that if you believe, you will see the glory of God?"
John 11:40, NIV

8

# Attacked...*The Power of the Blood of Jesus*

One evening when I was a teenager, I was out for a fun time with some friends from a Bible study group. One of the guys piped up and asked if anyone wanted to go two-tracking. Now, for some reading this who are from northern Michigan, you will know right away what that means. For those who are not as lucky to have enjoyed "God's country", let me explain. Northern Michigan is blessed with *a lot* of state lands comprised of woods and dirt trails. For fun, we hop in a car and drive those dirt trails to see what there is to see—this is two-tracking. Great adventures are to be had, and I was always up for an adventure! Unfortunately, no one else in the group wanted to join Jim and I, so we headed out in his little Beetle bug. (Yep, should have been my first red flag—Beetle bugs and dirt trails definitely don't mix!)

It was still daylight and I expected to be back before dark after a good couple of hours of fun. Jim and I were tootling around in the backwoods enjoying good conversation when he started following what looked like a trail but turned out to not be a trail. I can't explain how or why, but somehow, he got that Beetle bug straddled over a log laying across what wasn't a trail! As Jim became more and more agitated about our situation, he began to scare me. He got out of the car and slammed the door, kicking at the ground, and swearing that it was getting dark and we were stuck in the woods too far to walk out and no way to get help. Okay, so everyone gets a bit angry in situations like this, right?

When I started to get out of the car to evaluate the predicament we were in, Jim started screaming for me to get back in the car and to stay there, and that if I got out again, he was going to kill me—just a slight overreaction to the situation, you think? Was I scared? I was a little more than just uneasy about the turn of events. Jim got back in the car and started trying to rock the car off the log but to no avail. Again, he got out of the car and started screaming and kicking things around. I sensed that the only way out of this was to get Jim quieted down so he could think straight.

I asked him to get back in the car, which he did, and then I asked him to pray with me about our situation. This calmed him down enough to talk rationally. We came up with a plan to dislodge the Beetle bug from the log which was laying across the trail which wasn't a trail. We tried our plan, but it didn't work. Uh, oh. Once again, Jim got out of the car and started screaming and kicking the leaves, the ground, the car—anything and everything—all the while threatening me that he would kill me if I got out of the car. It is taking me seconds to type out what happened that night and seconds for you to read it. The reality is that what I've described to this point lasted for hours.

Jim got back in the car, pulled a glass bottle from under his seat, and started to take a drink. When I started to talk to him again, he slammed the glass bottle against the steering wheel and then proceeded to raise his arm to bring the broken glass down across my face. I raised my hand to block his and the glass cut the end of my finger. I hate to sound gory, but the truth is blood began to gush everywhere. I then again told Jim that we needed to pray. I had figured out this was the only thing that calmed him. After that prayer, Jim somehow managed to rock the Beetle bug enough that it came off the log and we were able to turn around and find a good two-track to get the heck out of those woods.

The nightmare continued as Jim would work himself into another "mood", stop the car and rant and rave. Each time, I would ask him to get back in the car, pray, and we would drive a little farther. Well into the night—or should I say wee hours of the morning—we finally made it out of the woods and onto a paved road. By this time, Jim was crazy and driving around 25 mph curves at 50 and 55 mph; so fast that the tires on my side of the car were no longer on the pavement, nor the shoulder of the road, but up on the side of the hill as we were flying around those Keystone Road curves!

By the grace of God, we finally made it into the town area. I recognized that we were near a mobile home park where a couple I knew lived, so I asked Jim to pull into the park and drop me off. My car was on the other side of town, but there was no way I wanted to be in that Beetle bug any longer. He pulled in, stopped the car, got out, and started smashing glass on the pavement again. I have no idea where he got this glass. By this time, I was exhausted from dealing with this maniac and wondering if I would be a statistic by sun up. It was then about 3:00 a.m., we had left our friends at about 7:30 p.m.

Again, Jim was threatening to kill me if I got out of the car, so I again asked him to get into the car so we could pray. He finally calmed down enough that he started driving. Soon we were near another friend's home, so I asked Jim to let me out there. I knew enough by now that I needed to have him pray with me before he got out of the car—he did. This time, I told him I would get out of the car, spend the rest of the night at my friend's and he would be able to go home and get some sleep since it was close to morning. To my surprise and jubilation he allowed me out of the car and he drove off. Yes!

In the morning, my friend drove me to my parents' home who then drove me to the hospital to have my finger bandaged. Jim showed up at our door later that morning asking my father what had happened. He explained that he had gone out to his car that morning and was scared because of the blood he saw everywhere. Obviously, my father did not invite him into the house for a cup of coffee—it was more like, if Jim didn't get off his property, he would be getting his gun. Jim never came around again, but I ran into him at a hospital years later. He explained to me that he was in rehab and that his actions that night were because of a flashback from using hard drugs. He was greatly sorry for the nightmare he had taken me through. I forgave him and told him I would pray for him because I knew he was up against a battle. (But I never hung out with him again!) What an experience!

But by the grace of God did I make it through that horror of a night! Through the years, I have looked at that scar on my finger and thought about that experience. I have come to understand a very powerful and meaningful thing. I don't hold anything against Jim. He had a battle to face just as we all have our own battles. As I continued to look at the scar on my finger, I came to realize that each drop of blood that gushed out of that wound had a purpose. If the dirt had been allowed to remain in the wound, it would have caused a painful infection—the spilling of the blood was to wash away the dirt.

The power is in the blood! "And he took the cup, and gave thanks, and gave it to them, saying, 'Drink ye all of it; for this is my blood of the new testament, which is shed for many for the remission of sins'" (Matthew 26:27-28, KJV). From Christ's crucifixion to the communion sacrament, the blood of Jesus has symbolized the cleansing of our sins. "In him we have redemption through his blood, the forgiveness of sins, in accordance with the riches of God's grace." (Eph 1:7, NIV).

We are forgiven and have gained the favor of our Creator God and are reclaimed from the enemy. "But if we walk in the light, as he is in the light, we have fellowship with one another, and the blood of Jesus, his Son, purifies us from all sin" (1 John 1:7, NIV). Our sins are cleansed from our record; our debt is paid, once and for all. "For you know that it was not with perishable things such as silver or gold that you were redeemed from the empty way of life handed down to you from your ancestors, but with the precious blood of Christ, a lamb without blemish or defect" (1 Peter 1:18-19, NIV). *Only* through Jesus!

There was a point in my life that I started getting out of line with God's will for my life and made very unwise choices. It is so easy to "cherry-pick" or twist His Word to justify our desires, but when we take His words and twist them, it doesn't change His truths; it merely allows the enemy to manipulate our minds to believe his lies and miss out on God's blessings and plan for our lives. After a while, I started to miss my close relationship with my Heavenly Father, but I believed Satan's lie that I had too much baggage—that I had failed God and wasn't good enough to kneel at God's feet and ask Him to once again forgive me. I couldn't see how He would want to take time for me now. Remember, Satan wants your soul just as much as Jesus does and he will lie, mimic God, and do whatever it takes to keep you in bondage. Such a simple choice—reject Jesus' truths and accept Satan's lies and bondage or reject Satan's lies and accept Jesus' truths and freedom.

God is not looking for perfection because we will not achieve that status until we reach heaven. He is looking for consistency: when we discover we have sinned, then consistently run to Him confessing and asking for His forgiveness.

> What do you think? If a man owns a hundred sheep, and one of them wanders away, will he not leave the ninety-nine on the hills and go to look for the one that wandered off? And if he finds it, truly I tell you, he is happier about that one sheep than about the ninety-nine that did not wander off.
>
> Matthew 18:12-13, NIV

It was at this point that I looked at the scar on my finger and I connected to the meaning of God's shed blood. As each drop of His blood spilled onto the ground, it was washing away the dirt from my wounded life—my life that had been separated from a relationship with God because of my dirt—my sin. Thank you, Jesus, for your great love that you were willing to have your blood shed so all of that dirt would be washed away and I could have the opportunity to be restored into a two-way relationship with my Heavenly Father once again! I ran—not walked—I ran, straight into the open arms of

Jesus and received the freedom to live and experience my Savior in the fullness of His glory.

Romans 8:15-16 confirms to us, "The Spirit you received does not make you slaves, so that you live in fear again; rather, the Spirit you received brought about your adoption to sonship. And by Him, we cry, 'Abba, Father.' The Spirit himself testifies with our spirit that we are God's children" (NIV).

Let me emphasize, I am not perfect, and that right there is proof of our Creator God's great love and grace! He knows my faults and shows them to me so that I can once again bring my life back into alignment with His truth. I've been through my "desert" many times just as the Israelites had to because, although God's child, my human nature is in a constant battle with my spiritual nature. It took a while for me to understand the warring natures, but God has remained by my side and protected and provided for me. The reality is that each time I make a wrong choice, He does not wash His hands of me but instead says, "Get up, take my hand! Together, you and I...I will bring you through!" God as my Creator knows my heart. My faith started with the first step in asking Him to forgive my sin.

# Epilogue

Consider that we are all terminal beginning from the second we are born...we just don't know when or how that last breath will come. We continue to live our earthly lives as though tomorrow is promised. Yet it is not. Eternity is promised, however! When we get news of a health issue, we spend thousands of dollars on medical expenses to prolong our earthly lives...how much more so we should be concerned about and investing in our spiritual life because eternity is forever! If we keep in mind our destination, we might live a little differently on the trip there.

It is not an accident that God has led me to share some of my experiences where He has proven to be more than a "fairy tale" and available to those who choose Him. Nor is it a coincidence that you are reading this book. Where do you see yourself in this truth about God's love for each one of us? Where do you fit in God's story? God loves you enough that He continues to pursue you, wherever you are. Confessing that we have sinned does not mean we are bad people, it simply acknowledges that we understand that sin fell on all of us because of Adam and Eve's choice. Even good people fall under this and need Jesus to experience restoration with God the Father. Has your free will choice stopped at just acknowledging that you believe in Him? Even Satan and his demons believe in Him. In fact, they tremble at His name! If you have not personally acknowledged and chosen to enter into a two-way relationship with Christ, He is waiting for you.

If you already know Him as your Lord, how deep are you willing to go to know Him even more? To what length does your faith extend? Are you living your faith at the capacity that God desires you to? Are you realizing the fullness of His blessings He has planned especially for you?

Are you ready to trust with a deeper faith and be even more victorious? Consider the depth of faith of Jehoshaphat and the people of Judah and Jerusalem.

After this, the Moabites and Ammonites with some of the Meunites came to wage war against Jehoshaphat. Some people came and told Jehoshaphat, "A vast army is coming against you from Edom, from the other side of the Dead Sea. It is already in Hazezon Tamar" (that is, En Gedi). Alarmed, Jehoshaphat resolved to inquire of the Lord, and he proclaimed a fast for all Judah. The people of Judah came together to seek help from the Lord; indeed, they came from every town in Judah to seek him.

Then Jehoshaphat stood up in the assembly of Judah and Jerusalem at the temple of the Lord in the front of the new courtyard and said: Lord, the God of our ancestors, are you not the God who is in heaven? You rule over all the kingdoms of the nations. Power and might are in your hand, and no one can withstand you. Our God, did you not drive out the inhabitants of this land before your people Israel and give it forever to the descendants of Abraham your friend? They have lived in it and have built in it a sanctuary for your Name, saying, 'If calamity comes upon us, whether the sword of judgment, or plague or famine, we will stand in your presence before this temple that bears your Name and will cry out to you in our distress, and you will hear us and save us.'

"But now here are men from Ammon, Moab and Mount Seir, whose territory you would not allow Israel to invade when they came from Egypt; so they turned away from them and did not destroy them. See how they are repaying us by coming to drive us out of the possession you gave us as an inheritance. Our God, will you not judge them? For we have no power to face this vast army that is attacking us. We do not know what to do, but our eyes are on you."

All the men of Judah, with their wives and children and little ones, stood there before the Lord. Then the Spirit of the Lord came on Jahaziel son of Zechariah, the son of Benaiah, the son of Jeiel, the son of Mattaniah, a Levite and descendant of Asaph, as he stood in the assembly. He said: "Listen, King Jehoshaphat and all who live in Judah and Jerusalem! This is what the Lord says to you: 'Do not be afraid or discouraged because of this vast army. For the battle is not yours, but God's. Tomorrow march down against them. They will be climbing up by the Pass of Ziz, and you will find them at the end of the gorge in the Desert of Jeruel. You will not have to fight this battle. Take up your positions; stand firm and see the deliverance the Lord will give you, Judah and Jerusalem. Do not be afraid; do not be discouraged. Go out to face them tomorrow, and the Lord will be with you.'"

Jehoshaphat bowed down with his face to the ground, and all the people of Judah and Jerusalem fell down in worship before the Lord. Then some Levites from the Kohathites and Korahites stood up and praised the Lord, the God of Israel, with a very loud voice.

Early in the morning they left for the Desert of Tekoa. As they set out, Jehoshaphat stood and said, "Listen to me, Judah and people of Jerusalem! Have faith in the Lord your God and you will be upheld; have faith in his prophets and you will be successful." After consulting the people, Jehoshaphat appointed men to sing to the Lord and to praise him for the splendor of his holiness as they went out at the head of the army, saying: "Give thanks to the Lord, for his love endures forever."

As they began to sing and praise, the Lord set ambushes against the men of Ammon and Moab and Mount Seir who were invading Judah, and they were defeated. The Ammonites and Moabites rose up against the men from

Mount Seir to destroy and annihilate them. After they finished slaughtering the men from Seir, they helped to destroy one another.

When the men of Judah came to the place that overlooks the desert and looked toward the vast army, they saw only dead bodies lying on the ground; no one had escaped. So Jehoshaphat and his men went to carry off their plunder, and they found among them a great amount of equipment and clothing and also articles of value—more than they could take away. There was so much plunder that it took three days to collect it. On the fourth day they assembled in the Valley of Berakah, where they praised the Lord. This is why it is called the Valley of Berakah to this day.

Then, led by Jehoshaphat, all the men of Judah and Jerusalem returned joyfully to Jerusalem, for the Lord had given them cause to rejoice over their enemies. They entered Jerusalem and went to the temple of the Lord with harps and lyres and trumpets. The fear of God came on all the surrounding kingdoms when they heard how the Lord had fought against the enemies of Israel. And the kingdom of

Jehoshaphat was at peace, for his God had given him rest on every side.

2 Chronicles 20:1-30, NIV

Be victorious, as Jehoshaphat as you seek to understand God's realness and plan for your life.

For the wages of sin is death, but the gift of God is eternal life in Christ Jesus our Lord.

Romans 6:23, NIV

For it is by grace you have been saved, through faith; and this is not from yourselves—it is the gift of God—

Ephesians 2:8, NIV

If you declare with your mouth, "Jesus is Lord," and believe in your heart that God raised him from the dead, you will be saved. For it is with your heart that you believe and are justified, and it is with your mouth that you profess your faith and are saved.

Romans 10:9-10, NIV

Jesus saith unto him, I am the way, the truth, and the life: no man cometh unto the Father, but by me.

John 14:6, KJV

Verily, verily, I say unto you, He that heareth my word, and believeth on him that sent me, hath everlasting life, and shall not come into condemnation; but is passed from death unto life.

John 5:24, KJV

As many as I love, I rebuke and chasten: be zealous therefore, and repent. Behold, I stand at the door, and knock: if any man hear my voice, and open the door, I will come in to him, and will sup with him, and he with me. To him that overcometh will I grant to sit with me in my throne, even as I also overcame, and am set down with my Father in his throne.

Revelation 3:20, KJV

We each have the free will choice to accept, believing in faith, the gift of restoration through Jesus, "The *true* fairy tale." It is up to each of us to accept the gift, open it, and enjoy the blessings God has planned especially for us.

I pray for you the Word from Ephesians 1:17-20 (KJV):

> That the God of our Lord Jesus Christ, the Father of glory, may give unto you the spirit of wisdom and revelation in the knowledge of him: The eyes of your understanding being enlightened; that ye may know what is the hope of his calling, and what the riches of the glory of his inheritance in the saints, and what is the exceeding greatness of his power to us-ward who believe, according to the working of his mighty power, which he wrought in Christ, when he raised him from the dead, and set him at his own right hand in the heavenly places.

# Afterword

Much prayer has gone into writing this book and God has been my guide throughout. When God first nudged me to begin writing down notes on some of the experiences during my journey with Him, I had no idea what would become of it. For Him to provide me the title of the book, *The TRUE Fairy Tale*, and wonder if or when a book would be written was also a struggle for me. I questioned whether other Christians would consider me a heretic for referring to God as the true "fairy tale". As I was completing the book, God confirmed to me that this was His story, and His title, and that I should leave it in His hands. One Sunday as I sat in church, I could not believe my ears when I heard the pastor use the words "fairy tale" referencing how some people perceive God. I knew immediately this was God's confirmation to the title. I submitted my initial manuscript with this title and left it in His hands.

Upon completion of the manuscript, I prayed God would provide the name of the publisher I was to submit it to. I asked a good friend, Linda, to also pray. The evening of the day I shared this need with Linda, I received a text from her with the information to Trilogy Publishing. She just "happened" to catch the information on a commercial. This also became a test of faith for me. I provided my contact information online and left two voicemails. Over the week in which I was waiting for someone to contact me, the devil continued to whisper to me that this must not be the right publishing company after all. I prayed that if it was, indeed, the right publisher, that they would contact me rather than me making any further attempts and that the person who did reach out to me would provide answers to my questions in a way that I would have peace.

When Stacy called, she was wonderful and we connected right away, confirming to me that Satan was just trying to keep me from God's purpose. Oh, how that sneaky devil tries in so many ways to divert us from the right path. I do not know whose hands this book will end up in, however, I trust that if even one reader is touched and comes to know God in a much more real way, then it has served its purpose. I am so totally in, with my whole heart, to serving His purpose for my life and continuing to go into even more "unfamiliar territory" as I continue my journey in His story, *The TRUE Fairy Tale*.

# Endnotes

(1) Genesis 1:26-31, KJV: [26] And God said, Let us make man in our image, after our likeness: and let them have dominion over the fish of the sea, and over the fowl of the air, and over the cattle, and over all the earth, and over every creeping thing that creepeth upon the earth. [27] So God created man in his own image, in the image of God created he him; male and female created he them.[28] And God blessed them, and God said unto them, Be fruitful, and multiply, and replenish the earth, and subdue it: and have dominion over the fish of the sea, and over the fowl of the air, and over every living thing that moveth upon the earth.[29] And God said, Behold, I have given you every herb bearing seed, which is upon the face of all the earth, and every tree, in the which is the fruit of a tree yielding seed; to you it shall be for meat.[30] And to every beast of the earth, and to every fowl of the air, and to every thing that creepeth upon the earth, wherein there is life, I have given every green herb

for meat: and it was so.[31] And God saw every thing that he had made, and, behold, it was very good. And the evening and the morning were the sixth day.

(2) Genesis 3, KJV: [1] Now the serpent was more subtil than any beast of the field which the LORD God had made. And he said unto the woman, Yea, hath God said, Ye shall not eat of every tree of the garden? [2]And the woman said unto the serpent, We may eat of the fruit of the trees of the garden: [3]But of the fruit of the tree which is in the midst of the garden, God hath said, Ye shall not eat of it, neither shall ye touch it, lest ye die. [4]And the serpent said unto the woman, Ye shall not surely die: [5]For God doth know that in the day ye eat thereof, then your eyes shall be opened, and ye shall be as gods, knowing good and evil. [6]And when the woman saw that the tree was good for food, and that it was pleasant to the eyes, and a tree to be desired to make one wise, she took of the fruit thereof, and did eat, and gave also unto her husband with her; and he did eat. [7]And the eyes of them both were opened, and they knew that they were naked; and they sewed fig leaves together, and made themselves aprons. [8]And they heard the voice of the LORD God walking in the garden in the cool of the day: and Adam and his wife hid themselves

from the presence of the LORD God amongst the trees of the garden. ⁹ And the LORD God called unto Adam, and said unto him, Where art thou? ¹⁰ And he said, I heard thy voice in the garden, and I was afraid, because I was naked; and I hid myself. ¹¹ And he said, Who told thee that thou wast naked? Hast thou eaten of the tree, whereof I commanded thee that thou shouldest not eat? ¹² And the man said, The woman whom thou gavest to be with me, she gave me of the tree, and I did eat. And the LORD God said unto the woman, What is this that thou hast done? And the woman said, The serpent beguiled me, and I did eat. ¹⁴ And the LORD God said unto the serpent, Because thou hast done this, thou art cursed above all cattle, and above every beast of the field; upon thy belly shalt thou go, and dust shalt thou eat all the days of thy life: ¹⁵ And I will put enmity between thee and the woman, and between thy seed and her seed; it shall bruise thy head, and thou shalt bruise his heel. ¹⁶ Unto the woman he said, I will greatly multiply thy sorrow and thy conception; in sorrow thou shalt bring forth children; and thy desire shall be to thy husband, and he shall rule over thee. ¹⁷ And unto Adam he said, Because thou hast hearkened unto the voice of thy wife, and hast eaten of the tree, of which I commanded thee, saying, Thou shalt not eat of it:

cursed is the ground for thy sake; in sorrow shalt thou eat of it all the days of thy life; ¹⁸ Thorns also and thistles shall it bring forth to thee; and thou shalt eat the herb of the field; ¹⁹ In the sweat of thy face shalt thou eat bread, till thou return unto the ground; for out of it wast thou taken: for dust thou art, and unto dust shalt thou return. ²⁰ And Adam called his wife's name Eve; because she was the mother of all living. ²¹ Unto Adam also and to his wife did the LORD God make coats of skins, and clothed them. ²² And the LORD God said, Behold, the man is become as one of us, to know good and evil: and now, lest he put forth his hand, and take also of the tree of life, and eat, and live for ever: ²³ Therefore the LORD God sent him forth from the garden of Eden, to till the ground from whence he was taken. ²⁴ So he drove out the man; and he placed at the east of the garden of Eden Cherubims, and a flaming sword which turned every way, to keep the way of the tree of life.

# About the Author

With a heart for young people, it is no surprise that Diane Mack dedicated herself to raising her son, Bryan, and daughter, Katie, which included homeschooling for many years. She also enjoyed mentoring many other young people over the years through various children's ministries at local churches. Diane served as the Capital Campaign Facilitator to build a local Christian High School now serving pre-school through 12th grade. Diane appreciates the many opportunities to travel, including to Germany; as well as having lived in Ohio, Michigan, Texas, New Mexico, Arizona, and Pennsylvania, establishing longtime friendships in all places. She and Bob currently reside in the Traverse City, Michigan area. If you would like to contact Diane, please email her at *TotallyIn.Him@gmail.com* or visit her Facebook page at TotallyIn-Him.

CPSIA information can be obtained
at www.ICGtesting.com
Printed in the USA
LVHW081055030920
664977LV00017B/1809

9 781647 732882